BO… …UCK

The only Comprehensive Potteries Companion you're ever going to need!

(includes an all new *Pottersaurus* !!)

Terry Bossons

Forward

"After much procrastination as to what to write as the forward for this book, I decided to ask a few of my heroes what they thought of my appetite for the area."
Terry Bossons 23/10/18

John Challis (**Boycie** in **Only Fools and Horses**):
"Terry Bossons has put Stoke on the map and I love going there to meet friends old and new"

Brian Nash (**Frankie goes to Hollywood**)
"What can I say about this man? If you cut him open he would bleed Stoke and Oatcakes. I am not an expert on oatcakes but I am an expert on Top Bananas and Terry is 24 carat Top Banana!"

Rick Witter (**Shed Seven**):
"What would Stoke be without Terry Bossons? What would Terry Bossons be without Stoke? God only knows. What I do know is that they fit like a well worn glove."

Ewen Macintosh (**Keith** in BBC's **The Office**):
"If you want to know who Mr. Stoke is then it's not Robbie Williams or Slash from Guns 'N Roses. They took the easy route out and moved to Hollywood. Mr. Stoke is Terry Bossons. He stayed behind to spend his life putting Stoke on the map. Some think this was a selfless act of community service and loyalty but the truth is he's just addicted to Oatcakes!"

Acknowledgements

Thanks to:

Malcolm Draper for the cover art.
Dan Townley for the 'Book not Buck' logo. (Even though he says 'Buck'!)
Dave Lee for the layout.
Adrian Tooth and **John Charles** for the illustrations.
Pete Conway for his local knowledge.
Dave Johnson for his dialect skills.
Jason Dale for those tales.
Trevor M, **Lee Fredericks**, **Kelvin Andrews** and **Mark Porter** for the DJ pages.
Alan Shaw for the Jimi Hendrix story.
Chris Burton for The Torch details.
Andy Ankers for The Theatre Royal info.
Danni Brownsill for The Sugarmill list.
Christian Patterson for the panto pages.
Nick Degg and **TVP** for the poems.

Plus the following people who helped make this happen:

Amy, Connor & Jaxxon Bossons, Ezra Townley, Kirst Leigh, Nick King, The Kismet, Dick Dale, Rob Fiddaman, Craig Longson, Callum Hanley, Ross Irving, Rich Hughes, Nick King, Alex Steventon, Roxanne Simmonds, Rob Ledgar, Dave Biff, Tor, Simon Donald, Maggot, Jesse McClure, Ewen Macintosh, Brian Nash, John Challis, Rick Witter, Arthur Bostrom, Rachel Shenton, Jon Acres, Liz Ellis, Louise Stones, Den Siegertsz and everyone at BBC Radio Stoke, Fred Hughes, 6 Towns Radio, Moorlands Radio, Stafford FM, Signal 1, Biddulph Chronicle, Eddie Hall, Dave Follows, Martin Tideswell and The Sentinel, Staffordshire University, Robbie Williams, Ernie Nuff, Slash, Uncle Ian Hudson, JLM, Yates, Reflex, Ollie and the Marland's, Stanley Muggins, Angela Newey, Terry Love, Moorland Pottery, Lonnie Cooke, Terry Blood, Mike Lloyd, Mel Scholes, Man of Fire, Alex Povey, Big Un, Bill Hardy, Average Joe, Gill Underwood, Talbie, Shaun Kelly, Jonathan Wilkes, The Regent, Phil Carr, John Williams, Ryan and Jack Dooley, John Stather, The Embrace Team, The Hewitts, Trevor & the guys at Tunster Market, June Cartwright & Our Burslem, Paul Rutter, Adam Finney, Alfie Dale, Annie Nash, Annette Brookes, Sherman & everyone who loves Staffordshire!

All information was collated from reliable sources. Any inaccuracies or spelling mistakes we can only apologise for. Permission to use photographs was asked for and I don't own the copyright for any including logos etc. – Terry Bossons

Thanks for the past and here's to the future!

In loving memory of my mum, **Edna Bossons** (1942-2018)

Famous Stokies

They were born and/or raised in Staffordshire...honest!

We all know Robbie Williams was born in Tunstall and Slash grew up in Blurton. But did you know these ten famous people lived here at one point?

Raphael Ravenscroft - Famous for the sax riff on the hit song 'Baker Street' by Gerry Rafferty. (Born In Stoke, 1954)

Dave Gorman - Comedian and TV presenter. (Born in Stafford, 1971)

Freddie Jones - Actor, recently played Sandy in Emmerdale and is father of BAFTA winning actor Toby Jones. (Born In Stoke-on-Trent, 1927)

Helen Baxendale - Played Emily in the hit US TV series Friends. (Not born here but grew up in Shenstone, Staffordshire in the 70s)

Jem Finer - Founder member of The Pogues and co-writer of 'A fairytale of New York. (Born in Stoke, 1955)

Adrian Rawlins - He played Harry Potter's dad James in the blockbuster movies. (Born In Stoke, 1958)

Ronnie Allen - Former England international and one of West Bromwich Albion's most famous footballers. (Born In Fenton, 1929)

Samuel Johnson - Writer of 'A dictionary of the English language'. (Born in Lichfield, 1709)

Fran Healy - Frontman of the massive indie band Travis. (Born In Stafford, 1973)

Levison Wood - Explorer who famously walked the entire length of The Nile. (Born in Hartshill, 1982)

Record shops we loved & lost

Once the staple of every high street, record shops used to be the life-blood in so many people's lives. They survived alongside much larger stores that also sold music (such as Woolworths, WH Smiths, John Menzies, and even Rumbelows).

Record shops didn't just sell records, they were a great place to hang out, listen to different styles of music, and meet like-minded souls.

Here are some that evolved in The Potteries:

Mike Lloyd's – Hanley & Newcastle
Replay - Tunstall
Protocol - Hanley
John Baddeley- Biddulph
Terry Blood - Hanley
Zodiac –Biddulph
Tony Denson Records - Newcastle
Lewis's - Hanley
Lonnie's - Stoke
Wildstyle - Hanley
Bevans - Longton
Ridgeways – Hanley
Bullet Records - Newcastle
Bews - Burslem
Sherwins - Hanley
Lotus - Hanley
Virgo - Burslem
Blaneys - Newcastle

You can still get vinyl records from:

Music Mania - Hanley
The Strand - Longton
Rubber Soul - Hanley
Global Groove - Hanley
Fish Records - Stone
Rhapsody - Tunstall

A CLOUD OF DUST By Dave Johnson

In the days before proper cleaning machines were brought in, the floors in the 'clay end' would be thick with clay dust – not very good from a health point of view, so the workers had to clean up as best they could at the end of the shift.

Obviously when you try to sweep a floor covered in clay dust, it would resemble a foggy day and make it even more of a health hazard, so the idea was to get a bucket of sawdust and get it under the tap so that the water was soaked up by the contents.

If the wet sawdust was sprinkled about randomly on the floor, then that would help keep the dust down, but that didn't seem to register with everybody.

Bill was a dishmaker, who had a young lad named Dennis labouring for him. As the working day drew to an end, Bill asked Dennis to get a bucket of sawdust and then sweep up for him while he nipped to the toilet. When Bill returned, he found could hardly see two yards in front of him, the dust was that thick.

Stumbling upon Dennis, he said: "I told you to use sawdust."

The young lad replied: "I did."

Bill: "Wet sawdust, not dry you idiot."

Dennis: "There wasn't any wet sawdust."

The lad, green around the ears didn't realise all he needed to do was add water to the bucket."

Ten iconic Stoke City games

10. (2-0) Man City 2015 (Stoke tear apart the billionaire league leaders at The Brit)
9. (0-0) Ajax 1974 - UEFA Cup (Stoke almost topple the European darlings at the Olympic Stadium)
8. (1-0) Stockport 1992 - Autoglass Final (A Wembley victory revives the club)
7. (1-0) Notts County 1979 (A late winner gives Stoke a dramatic promotion to the top-flight)
6. (3-2) Villa 2008 (First home game thriller sets bar for 10-year Premier League stay)
5. (10-3) West Brom 1937 Victoria Ground (Record league victory)
4. (5-0) Arsenal 1970 (Destroying the team that would win the double later the same season)
3. (6-1) Liverpool 2015 (Steven Gerrard's last game for The Reds turns into a bloody – albeit hilarious - nightmare)
2. (5-0) Bolton FA Cup semi-final 2011 (Underdogs win the perfect game at Wembley)
1. (2-1) Chelsea League Cup Final 1972 (Major silverware in a thrilling Wembley final)

Thanks to David Lee (author of the book "Stoke City's Greatest Games") for compiling this list. His new book "Premier! Stoke City's 10 Years In The Premier League" is now available.

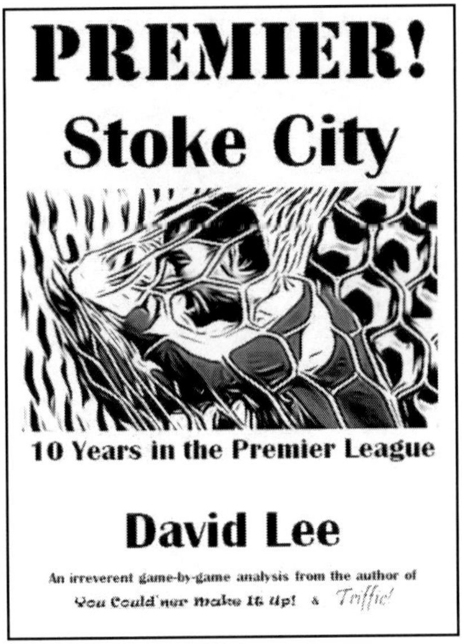

FREE COOKING By Dave Johnson

The "glost kiln" was where the second firing took place, the first being the "biscuit kiln." When the ware emerged from the gloss kiln it resembled the finish article, but without the pattern, which when added would go through the final firing process in the "enamel kiln."

On the noon shift or on the night shift, when there were fewer bosses about – and with the lack of canteen facilities, the glost kiln was the place to be if you fancied a hot meal during your break.

When a kiln truck came out of the kiln, the temperatures were much too hot to touch, and protective gloves had to be worn, but as the ware cooled a little, you could take out a plate (still hot) and place a couple of rashers of bacon on it, and as they were cooking, crack open an egg and add the contents to the plate.

The heat would help cook the meal in no time, so you would just get a few rounds of bread from within your locker and hey presto, a hot meal!

10 DJ performances of note in Stoke-on-Trent

1. **Derrick May** - Sindrome at Shelleys 1990
2. **Sasha** NYE - Delight at Shelleys 1991
3. **Dust Bros** (Chemical Bros) - Golden at The Void 90s
4. **Carl Cox/Pete Tong/Sasha** - Golden's 8th birthday at The Void 2000
5. **Armand Van Helden** & **Fatboy Slim** - Trentham Gardens 1999
6. **Kool DJ Herc** - Satchmos 2000
7. **Grandmaster Flash** - Satchmos 2001
8. **Seth Troxler** - The Move at The Sugarmill 2015
9. **Dimitri From Paris** - The Move at The Sugarmill 2016
10. **Skream** - The Move at The Sugarmill 2018

Thanks to DJ and Event organiser Lee Fredericks for helping to compile this list.

Pete Conway's mate Radar

Pete has a mate called Radar. He was given that nickname due to his resemblance to the character "Radar" in the TV show MASH.

Radar was in Las Vegas to see Gladys Knight with his friend a few years ago.

As she was doing the encore "Midnight train to Georgia", she came down into the audience. She went up to a table & asked where they were from. One of them replied, "New York", so Gladys said, "Let's have a big cheer for New York!"

The next table were from Chicago so she got a big cheer for Chicago.

She then came over to Radar's table and asked:
"Where are you from?"
Radar said "Hanley."
Gladys said, "Let's have a cheer for Hanley!"
Radar's mate said to him "Why did you say Hanley, you're from Sneyd Green!"
Radar replied "I didn't think she would of heard of Sneyd Green!"

10 DJ performances of note in Stoke-on-Trent

1. **Derrick May** - Sindrome at Shelleys 1990
2. **Sasha** NYE - Delight at Shelleys 1991
3. **Dust Bros** (Chemical Bros) - Golden at The Void 90s
4. **Carl Cox/Pete Tong/Sasha** - Golden's 8th birthday at The Void 2000
5. **Armand Van Helden** & **Fatboy Slim** - Trentham Gardens 1999
6. **Kool DJ Herc** - Satchmos 2000
7. **Grandmaster Flash** - Satchmos 2001
8. **Seth Troxler** - The Move at The Sugarmill 2015
9. **Dimitri From Paris** - The Move at The Sugarmill 2016
10. **Skream** - The Move at The Sugarmill 2018

Thanks to DJ and Event organiser Lee Fredericks for helping to compile this list.

Pete Conway's mate Radar

Pete has a mate called Radar. He was given that nickname due to his resemblance to the character "Radar" in the TV show MASH.

Radar was in Las Vegas to see Gladys Knight with his friend a few years ago.

As she was doing the encore "Midnight train to Georgia", she came down into the audience. She went up to a table & asked where they were from. One of them replied, "New York", so Gladys said, "Let's have a big cheer for New York!"

The next table were from Chicago so she got a big cheer for Chicago.

She then came over to Radar's table and asked:
"Where are you from?"
Radar said "Hanley."
Gladys said, "Let's have a cheer for Hanley!"
Radar's mate said to him "Why did you say Hanley, you're from Sneyd Green!"
Radar replied "I didn't think she would of heard of Sneyd Green!"

Christian Patterson and Panto

Favourite current local saying: "He's a Comical Dick!"

Here is a list of the pantomimes Jonathan Wilkes has starred in at The Regent Theatre in Hanley:

2005: Mother Goose
2006: Aladdin
2007: Cinderella (Christian Patterson started this year)
2008: Snow White
2009: Dick Whittington (Pete Conway appeared)
2010: Robinson Crusoe
2011: (the year Joe Swash did it)
2012: Cinderella
2013: Snow White
2014: Dick Whittington
2015: Peter Pan
2016: Cinderella
2017: Aladdin
2018: Robin Hood
2019: Mother Robinson Whittington & the 7 Merry Cats ??!?

Daft Punk in Staffordshire

Known worldwide as pioneers of dance music, Daft Punk did a gig here in the late 90s. Local DJ & producer - Kelvin Andrews sorted this out and told me the story:

"They were so young, totally unheard of at the time. After soundchecking at Keele University, they spent the day asking what records I was playing . Back at my house they spent hours going through my racks and talking in French. Only Thomas could speak English. They came to play because Soma Records in Glasgow had put out Da Funk and I used to end my sets with it. The label contacted me and asked if I'd put them on somewhere.

There were only about 25 people who turned up on that night, but Thomas asked the label to contact me again to do another show. This time there were 500 locked outside a sold-out Keele.

The Trent Vale Poet

"Fenton"

I wer' born in Fenton
And there I'll get me pension
I'll not stray, I'll always stay
Cos I wer' born in Fenton

I went t' school in Fenton
I had the cane, I got detention
I'll not leave, I'll live, I'll breathe
The giddy air of Fenton

I wer' wed in Fenton
To a girl from Fenton
We had a kid, named him Sid
The b******d moved to Longton

The Kismet

Established in 1962, The Kismet was the first Indian restaurant in Staffordshire.
Owner Ala Uddin Ahmed brought his family to Stoke-on-Trent from Bangladesh to start the venture.

They opened their restaurant in a building made famous by Potteries' novelist Arnold Bennett, 1/1a Queen Street, which was the Steam Printing Works in Bennett's novel The Clayhanger. The three storey building stands proud at the junction of Queen Street and Waterloo Road, looking like Wedgwood's Big House's less well-off cousin.

Robbie Williams and Phil Taylor have dined there on numerous occasions and it's still run by the same family.

www.kismetstoke.com

The Torch.

The Torch is known for its amazing Northern Soul nights but did you know the following bands and artists played there?

Amen Corner
Black Sabbath
T Rex
Major Lance
The Drifters
The Stylistics
Arthur Connelly
Inez & Charlie Fox
The Kinks
Al Green

Thanks to Chris Burton (owner of The Torch) for the list.

We asked Chris Burton what night stands out for him from the list and he said: "Arthur Connelly's toupee fell off during his performance; he just picked it up and placed it back on! Then he continued as if nothing had happened!"

Jollees Legends

Many a famous star has rocked up in Longton to entertain a full house whilst they tuck into their chicken in a basket. Here are some of the biggest names:

JOLLEES

Tommy Cooper
Cilla Black
Bob Monkhouse
Gene Pitney
Cliff Richard
Morecambe and Wise
Matt Monroe
Norman Wisdom
Lulu
Tommy Steele

Did you go to Jollees? Who did you see? Email: booknotbuck@gmail.com

CILLA BLACK

Wed 28th, Thur 29th, Fri 30th, Sat 31st JAN . 1981

GOLD : Wed £3.50., Thur £3.50., Fri £4.25., Sat £4.50.

SILVER : Wed £3.00., Thur £3.00., Fri £3.75., Sat £4.00.

Tommy Cooper

My dad saw Tommy Cooper at Jollees...

He was doing a magic trick and asked for my dad's watch.... He put it in a bag and smashed it up. Then he moved onto another trick. At the end of the show my dad asked about his watch. Tommy said it's in that bag in a thousand pieces. Dad said OK so where's the magic. Tommy admitted there wasn't any.... But he was staying in a hotel nearby and invited the family for tea the next day. They all went and Tommy recommended the steak pie. My dad ordered that and you will never guess what was inside it....?

Steak!

[In memory of Alfie Dale]

Molly Leigh - The Burslem Witch?

"Molly Leigh, Molly Leigh, Chase me around the apple tree."

Margaret Leigh aka Molly Leigh was believed to have been born in 1685 and lived on the outskirts of Burslem. Because of her ugly appearance, she was called a witch by a lot of the townspeople. Local pastor - Reverend Thomas Spencer agreed that she must be a witch because she refused to go to church.

With no family around, her only friend and companion was her pet Blackbird. Molly died of natural causes and was buried at St. John's Church, Burslem on 1st April 1741. The blackbird is said to have caused a nuisance afterwards so was captured and put into the same grave.

The grave is laid North to South so is easy to spot. People still visit today but dare they utter the legend "Molly Leigh, Molly Leigh, Chase me around the apple tree."?

Lobby

"Lobby on the hob" Nick Degg

You are my Winter
Swaddling me in Love
To keep out the chill
Lobby on the hob

You are my Spring
Tulip yellow dresses
Bare arms, holding hands
Corn on the cob

You are my Summer
Birdsong mornings
Lazy afternoons
Salad days

You are my Autumn
Golden hues
You really suit a hat
Lobby on the hob.

Ten Iconic Port Vale matches

1. (2-0) Blackpool - 20/2/54 FA Cup 5th round, Vale knock out the holders that include Sir Stanley Matthews. Port Vale went on to the semi-final but lost to West Brom.
2. (2-1) Tottenham - 30/1/1988 FA Cup 4th round. Ray Walker scored a world class goal to beat the top flight stars.
3. (3-1) Stoke City - 24/11/92 FA Cup first round. A game famous for the ball getting stuck in the mud when Dave Regis thought he had scored.
4. (2-1) Stockport - 22/5/93 Autoglass trophy final. Vale triumph in their first ever visit to Wembley.
5. (2-1) Brentford - 22/4/2001 - LDV Final. Victory at The Millennium stadium for Brian Horton's men.
6. (2-1) Everton - 14/2/96 - FA Cup 4th round replay - Bogie and McCarthy make it a St. Valentine's Day Massacre.
7. (7-1) Burton Albion - 05/04/2013 - Vale edged closer to promotion with seven goals including a Lee Hughes hat trick.
8. (3-1) Brighton - 07/05/95 - The Valiants gain promotion after disappointment in the play-off final the previous year.
9. (1-1 but lost on penalties) Arsenal - 14/01/98 - Vale take an Arsenal team to penalties that includes Bergkamp, Seaman, Wright, Vieira and Anelka.
10. (4-4) QPR - 20/01/97 - QPR came back from being 0-4 down at half time to grab a draw.

Thanks to the Wonder of Port Vale Facebook group for their help putting together this list.

Dales Tales

Not only is Jason Dale one of our best loved local entertainers, he knows more Staffordshire yarns than most. We picked his brains for some priceless Potteries parables (and Newcastle-Under-Lyme nuggets).

#1

BLACK SABBATH, THE GRATEFUL DEAD. MUNGO JERRY & SCREAMING LORD SUTCH AT THE UK VERSION OF WOODSTOCK.... IN NEWCASTLE UNDER LYME 1970

Not many people realise, but one of the first ever major UK Rock Festivals took place in Newcastle Under Lyme. It promised to rival the Woodstock Festival in The U.S. and The Grateful Dead performed their first ever UK show there.

The Hollywood Music Festival was held at Leycett in an area called Hollywood on the grounds of Ted Askey's (pig) Farm at Finney Green, between Madeley Heath and Leycett, near Newcastle, Staffordshire, on 23 & 24 May 1970. It was notable not only for that first performance of The Grateful Dead in the UK but also for the performance of Mungo Jerry, and such notable bands as Free, Ginger Baker's Air Force, Colosseum, Family, Black Sabbath & Traffic.

The festival has generally tended to be eclipsed by the larger, better known festival of 1970 - the Isle of Wight Festival

Some of the

Most memorable gigs in Staffordshire ever!

(In no particular order)

Oasis - Wheatsheaf, Stoke 11/04/94

Mott The Hoople (supported by **Queen**) - Victoria Hall, Hanley 18/11/73

David Bowie - Top Rank, Hanley 07/09/72

Libertines - Underground, Hanley 21/04/04

U2 - Victoria Hall, Hanley 04/03/83 (or Keele 29/11/80)

The Beatles - Trentham Gardens (one of many local shows) 11/10/63

Slash - Victoria Hall, Hanley 24/07/11

Bon Jovi - Britannia Stadium, Trentham 23/08/2000

INXS - Victoria Hall, Hanley 23/07/93

Motorhead and **Ozzy Osbourne** - Vale Park, Burslem 01/08/81

Peter Green (with **Cozy Powell** on drums) - Wheatsheaf, Stoke 24/09/96

Cat Stevens)supported by **Engelbert**

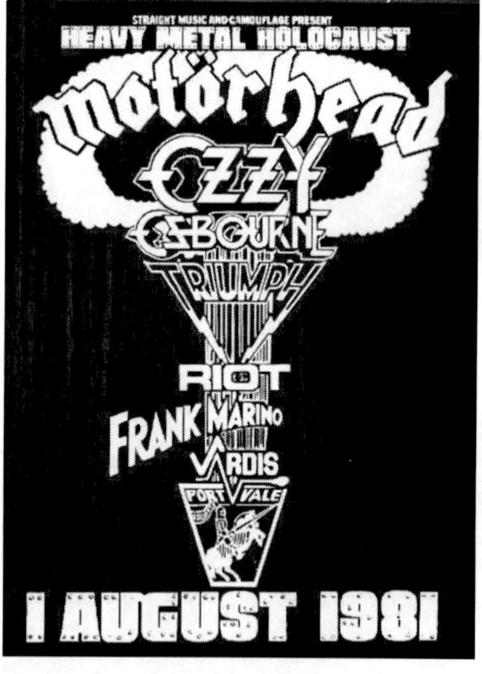

Humperdinck and **Jimi Hendrix**) - The Gaumont Hanley 23/04/67

Led Zeppelin - Trentham Gardens - 05/01/73

Eric Clapton - Victoria Hall, Hanley 28/11/78

Rolling Stones - Leek Town Hall 24/12/63

Blur - The Academy, Hanley 27/05/93

The Specials (supported by **Madness**) - Victoria Hall, Hanley 31/10/79

Moby - Lomax, Stoke 21/11/02

Ed Sheeran, Keele Uni 18/10/2011

The Clash - Victoria Hall, Hanley 13/07/82 (or 18/06/80)

Climax Blues Band (supported by **Squeeze**, their first gig outside London) - Victoria Hall, Hanley 10/09/75

Who have I missed off this list?
email: booknotbuck@gmail.com

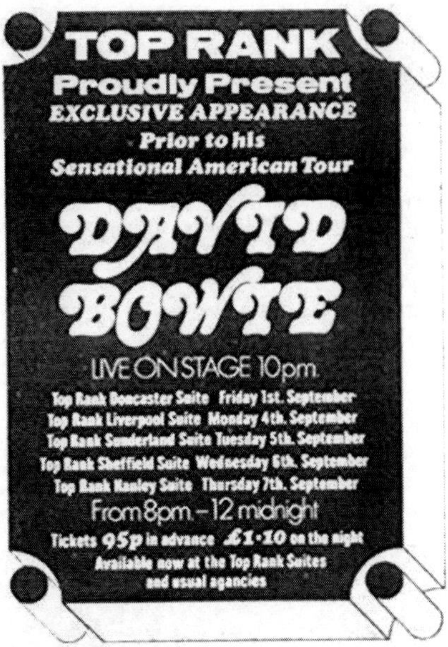

On the beat

Former policeman, Alan Shaw was at The Gaumont in Hanley on Sunday 23rd April 1967 with his sergeant on a supervisory visit. In the corridor of the venue was the one and only Jimi Hendrix with his band. He asked if there was any way of getting a bottle and Alan said he could sort it (even though it was a Sunday and they had strict licensing laws in those days). A quick trip to the back door of The Unicorn pub up the road and the officer was able to secure a bottle of Johnny Walkers scotch for a couple of quid.

Hendrix gave Alan a 10 pound note and he kept the change (about £150 today)...maybe because Jimi never offered him a swig!

Sugarmill gigs

A few of today's biggest bands have stopped off to play in Hanley on their rise to fame. Here are a few that have performed at The Sugarmill in recent years:

22.02.00 - Muse
29.03.00 - Coldplay (supporting Terris)
12.09.04 - Kasabian
17.04.07 - Biffy Clyro
10.07.07 - The National
19.10.08 - Bring Me The Horizon
30.11.12 - Foals
22.09.13 - The 1975
22.05.14 - Wolf Alice
05.12.14 - Catfish and The Bottlemen
05.03.16 - Blossoms
03.04.17 - Idles

Nightclubs:

Here we showcase some great local nightclubs that are now a distant memory. Did you meet your partner in any of these?

The Place/Rosie's - Hanley
Mr Smiths/Roxy Roller Rink/Joel's/20s/Academy/The Void - Hanley
Beer Keller/Robertaux/Excalibur/Freetown/The Club - Hanley
Sammi Belles/Maxims - Newcastle - Hanley
The Highwayman - Threapwood
Top Rank/Baileys - Hanley
Inset - Stoke
Satchmos - Hanley
Grouchos/Jaxx - Hanley
Queens - Basford
Liquid - Hanley
Fluid - Hanley
Jumpin Jaks - Hanley
Gaiety - Hanley
Brannigans - Festival Park
Teddy's - Trentham
The Torch - Tunstall
Shelleys - Longton
Satchmos - Hanley
Flickers/Flares/Zero - Hanley
Savoy/Metropolis - Newcastle
Regimes/Uropa - Hanley
Heavy Steam Machine - Hanley
Vale Social/Valiants - Burslem
Crafty Cockney - Smallthorne

The Grovesnor - Burslem
Jollees/Leisurebowl - Longton
Embassy Club/007/Heaven and Hell- Burslem
Penny Farthing/Maxims/Chico's - Hanley
Crystal/Tiffany's/Ritzy/Fatties/Zanzibar/The Cube - Newcastle
Top of the world/Reynolds Bar - Stafford
Liberty's/Locker Room - Hanley
Hudson's - Newcastle
Mystiques - Hanley
Adulte/Mayfair - Burslem
Top Rank/Baileys - Hanley
Inset - Stoke
Yogi's - Newcastle
Apollo - Longton
Bunker 13 - Hanley
Cuba - Hanley
Bobo's/Strikes - Burslem
JFK/Cheeky Disco - Hanley
Zenn/Touch - Hanley
Lomax - Stoke
Chaplins - Hanley
Time and Space - Newcastle
Spots - Knypersley
Lautrecs - Weston Coyney

Thanks for all the guys on Facebook who helped build this list. If you can think of anymore or have any stories please email bookorbuck@gmail.com

Theatre Royal

Andy Ankers started work at the Theatre Royal in 1983 (aged 9), and he was there till it sadly closed down. We asked him for one story from his time at the legendary venue.

The very first pantomime I got to work on was Aladdin. This was in December 1983, and I was only 10. But I was able to help out front of house with my mum selling programmes. I used to sell more than most other people as people thought I was cute so bought off me instead of someone else.

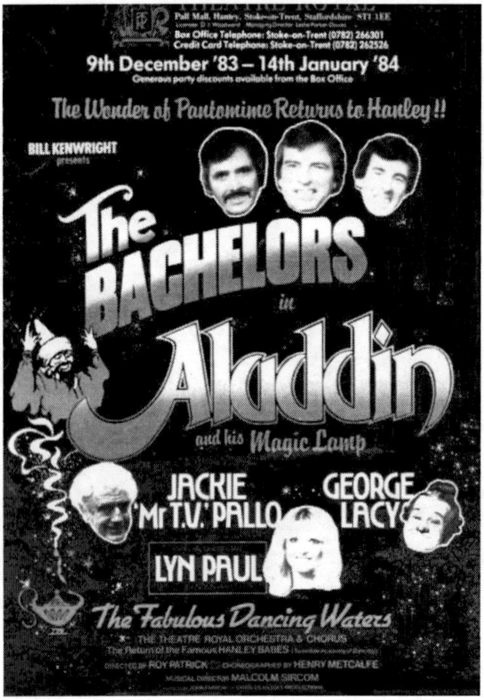

The panto had some legendary names (most I had never heard of) apart from one: Mr TV himself Jackie Pallo, the wrestler. I used to watch him on a Saturday on ITV and loved him. He was playing the baddie which meant we could boo and hiss as much as we liked.

We had watched a few rehearsals, and couldn't wait to see the show open. The first night came, the main theatre curtains were down and the band started to play the overture; it was electric. The curtain went up & you saw a layer of dry ice all over the stage. Jackie got his evil music and made a slow walk forward to his rehearsed spot. All the audience booed and hissed and the noise was deafening. He took a massive breath in to utter his first line……. and passed out!

He had breathed too much of the dry ice in and caused him to pass out. The curtain came straight back in and an announcement was made.

About 10 minutes later the band were cued to start again, the curtain raised and as he walked forward he got the biggest cheer of all the night. And every time he came on nobody booed or hissed at him at all and went from the biggest villain to the biggest hero for one night only.

Pubs we have lost

A list of pubs that have called last orders for good in Staffordshire

Top 'oth Trent - Biddulph
Out of Town - Birches Head
The Sperling - Norton
Riley's - High Lane
Foaming Quart - Burslem
New Queen - Cobridge
Continental Bar - Hanley
Evergreens - Cobridge
Pig and Whistle - Bucknall
Shades - Birches Head
The Shamrock - Longton
The Hillberry - Bucknall
Hickories - Longton
O'Learys - Stoke
The Globe - Bucknall
The Victoria - Fenton
Albert Inn - Northwood
The Royal Oak - Fenton
Bell and Bear - Shelton
Heath's - Hanley
The Corner Cupboard- Shelton
Manhattan Bar - Hanley
Carmountside - Abbey Hulton
The Dew Drop - Hanley
The Red Lion - Burslem
The Red Lion - Bucknall
The Duke of Wellington - Fenton
The Swan - Stoke
Miner's Arms - Fenton
The Roebuck - Shelton
The Top Vine - Longton
The Newtown - Fenton
The Ivy House - Hanley
.The Waterloo - Longton.
The Cross Keys - Northwood
The Bottom' Vine - Longton

Borough Exchange - Hanley
Hope and Anchor - Chell
Black Horse - Hanley
Bird in Hand - Etruria
The Antelope - Hanley
Sutherland Arms - Newcastle.
Spring Cottage - Bentilee
Leadbellys - Hanley
London Road Tavern - Newcastle
Left Bank - Hanley
Robin Hood - Longton
The Ancient Britain - Tunstall
Yates's - Hanley
The Mitre - Burslem
Trinity's - Hanley
The Thurston - Bucknall
Flickers - Hanley
The Greenway - Baddeley Green
The Three Tuns - Hanley
The American - Cobridge
Park Inn - Burslem
The Goose - Stanfields
The Bush - Smallthorne
Queens Head - Tunstall
Woodshutts - Kidsgrove
The Hop Inn - Sandyford
Elephant and Castle - Chell
The Matador - Knypersley
The Ford - Smallthorne
The New Black Bull -Brindley Ford
Brassingtons - Newcastle
The Locker Room - Hanley
The Gardeners Rest - Brindley Ford
Lloyd's Tavern - Burslem
Holden Bridge - Holden Bridge
Duke of Bridgewater - Longport
The Railway - Longport
Norma Jean's - Festival Park

This is not a definitive list, so if you want to submit a pub that you miss please email: bookorbuck@gmail.com

Trevor M's Top 10

We asked DJ legend, Trevor M what were the biggest songs he spun at The Place Nightclub.

the place
HANLEY
The Greatest Place in the World

1. Keni Burke - Let somebody love you
2. D'train you're the one for me
3. Geraldine Hunt - Can't fake the feeling
4. Vicky D - This beat is mine
5. SOS Band - The Finest
6. Carl Anderson - Buttercup
7. Glenn Jones - I'm somebody
8. The Crusaders- Street Life
9. Change - you are my melody
10. William DeVaughn - Be thankful for what you got

He said "On a different day I could find another 10 but these would always be in my box. Very difficult to give a definitive 10."

Dales Tales

#2.

The River Trent (Where did the name 'Trent' come from?)

The name "Trent" is from a Celtic word possibly meaning "strongly flooding". More specifically, the name may be a contraction of two Celtic words, tros ("over") and hynt ("way"). This may indeed indicate a river that is prone to flooding.

A traditional but almost certainly wrong opinion is that of Izaak Walton, who states in The Complete Angler (1653) that the Trent is "... so called from thirty kind of fishes that are found in it."

The River Trent (Prehistoric)
Prehistory
During the Pleistocene epoch (1.7 million years ago), the River Trent rose in the Welsh hills. Imagine what our accent would have been like had it stayed that way??!!

Pot Banks

Pot Banks were everywhere in Staffordshire, employing thousands of people until recent times. Thankfully our pottery is still of great value and loads of Pot Banks and smaller operations are still going strong. Here are a few examples:

Emma Bailey - Middleport
Emma Bridgewater - Hanley
Steelite - Middleport
Valentine's Clays - Stoke
Burleigh - Middleport
Bairstow - Birches Head
Wedgwood - Barlaston
Wade - Etruria
Moorcroft - Burslem
Eden Fine China - Longton
Foley - Longton

If you want to see how pottery is made or look at its history, visit Gladstone Pottery Museum in Longton or Middleport Pottery.

http://www.stokemuseums.org.uk/gpm/
http://www.middleportpottery.org

Celebrity Oatcake Fillings

Nick Hancock- Cheese, tomatoes and bacon in the morning, raspberry jam at tea time.
Peter Crouch - Bacon and cheese
Jackie Trent - Best butter
Wendy Turner-Webster - Soya baser cheese, mushrooms and tomatoes
Adrian 'Jackpot' Lewis - Bacon and cheese
Phil 'The Power' Taylor - Sausage and fried egg
Jonathan Wilkes - Bacon, cheese and tinned tomatoes
Pete Conway - Sausage, cheese with fruity sauce.
Jesse McClure - Bacon, cheese and brown sauce
Glen Matlock (Sex Pistols) - Bacon and cheese

Dales Tales

#3

Did you know there is a Bronze Age Cemetery In Stoke?

Barrow Cemetery in Stoke On Trent, Staffordshire.

A Bronze Age barrow group which includes the bowl barrows preserved up to 1.2m of height. The first barrow is on the crest of the hill above, about 1 metre tall, from here we can see the biggest barrow and the built upon barrow and further on the smallest barrow with the hilltop trig point .The biggest barrow has the obligatory scooped interior and a fenced off tree.

The strangest of the group has no grass covering, instead a concrete floor from some modern construction, despite it's modern appearance it really is a bronze age barrow. Further on is the smallest barrow about 3ft tall then it's down and up a small valley to the trig point and a great view marred slightly by three big quarries.

Finding them: A small lane heads south off the A52 to the little village of Wooton, after passing Weaver farm a small car park appears on the right , a footpath goes to the trig point 371m high. This is the last Peak Hill before descending onto the Staffordshire plain (though it's outside the national park).

Mark Porter's Top 10 at the Place in Hanley

1. **N Trance – Set You Fre**e - a classic feel good song that used to make The Place go into meltdown. I remember turning the volume down and the noise of everyone singing was just incredible.

2. **Bobby Brown – Two Can Play That Game** – a floor filler that would still get them dancing now, was a cross over from Cheese to Dance so it was loved by most.

3. **Oceanic – Insanity** - this was probably the tune that defined the early 90's, the Dream Tripper mix was the version I played in The Place. It was a popular tune that really went down well. Probably the tune that changed the music style from the 80's into the 90's

4. **Snap – Rhythm is a Dance**r – possibly one of the biggest floor fillers of the early 1990's that was guaranteed to get the dance floor full, playing the extended version was a total new style of music. Feel good for The Place, this became an iconic track.

5. **New Order – Blue Monda**y – one of the most played tracks in The Place, it didn't matter if it was a remix or the original. Play this today, close your eyes and you're back there in The Place - absolute classic tune.

6. **Tag Team – Whoomp (There it Is)** – just a tune that was that feel good weekend song, everyone sang along and it became a real classic. One all the DJ's in The Place used to play.

7. **Rufus & Chaka Khan – Ain't Nobody** - most people will remember that at ten to two we ended the night with some slow tunes. This was the crossover tune that took us down into the mellow bit ready for the slow dances. It was quite funny watching the guys walking round the floor looking for someone to dance with, I often wonder how many people were thrown together following this. Did we help to increase the baby boom, who knows but it was a great end to the night.

8. **Steve Silk Hurley – Jack Your Body** – this tune will always be the one that bought the house sound of Chicago into The Place. I first played this in The Place in 1986 it really changed the direction of the music and bought

us on from the 80s disco and New Wave. Break Dancing became more techno and so Dance Music was born.

9. **Grandmaster Flash & Melle Mel & The Furious Five - White Lines (Don't Don't Do It**) Original Long Version – this is another classic from the 80s that stayed as a floor filler right through The Place years until the day it closed. It was an iconic tune. I remember this was at one point one of the most requested songs we had in The Place.

10. **Faithless – Insomnia** – in my top 10 I have saved probably the best until last, the most Iconic song ever to have been played at The Place in my opinion. The Monster Mix of this track is absolutely incredible. It sure is possibly one of the greatest dance tracks of all time. It is a tune that doesn't age and the younger generation of today would love this. It is an incredible piece and to me is a work or art. This is a floor filler, it was so hard to write my top 10 as there are so many wonderful tunes that could be included in this: Baby D, Dee Lite, Kariya, but to me these tunes are worthy of being in the top 10.

The saddest part for me is the younger generation will never experience The Place - the venue that for me was a part of Stoke on Trent's heritage as much as anything! We built this city on Music, Clay & Coal.

The Baytles

Imagine if The Beatles were from Stoke and not Liverpool? What if they recorded their songs in Abbey Hulton not at Abbey Road? Potteries dialect expert Dave Johnson has come up with a list of songs by The Baytles!

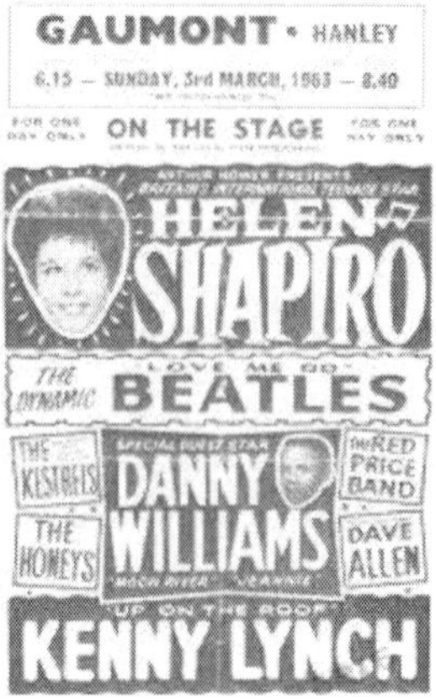

Yesterday – Yesdee
I Feel Fine - Ar Fale Farn
Nowhere Man – Noweer Mon
She Loves You – Er Luvs Thay
Twist and Shout – Twist und Shite
Come Together – Cum Gether
A Day In The Life – A Dee In Th'larf
I Am The Walrus – Arm Th'Wall Russ
Hello Goodbye – Ayup, Say Thee
Yellow Submarine – Yeller Submrane
Ain't She Sweet – Inner Her Swayte
A Hard Day's night – Ard Dees Nayte
We Can Work It Out – Way Cun Werkeet Ite
Can't Buy Me Love – Conner Buy May Luv
Magical Mystery Tour – Majeecle Mistry Toor
Strawberry Fields Forver – Strawbry Faylds Frever
I Want To Hold Your Hand – Ar Wanner Owd Thar And
With A Little Help From My Friends – With A Birrer Relp From Me Mates
Things We Said Today – Thins Way Sed Terdee
Fool On The Hill – Foal On Thill
Old Brown Shoe – Ode Brine Show
All My Loving – Aller Mar Luveen
Drive My Car - Drarve Mar Car
Get Back – Goo Awee
I'm Down – Arm Dine
Let It Be – Lerreet Bay

KING'S HALL, STOKE № 64
SATURDAY, JAN., 26TH

Midland Entertainments and Rockstar Enterprises present
Hit Recorders of "LOVE ME DO"
THE BEATLES
7-45 — 11-45 p.m.

Licensed Bar Buffet Late Buses TICKETS : 6/-
No admission after 10 p.m.

Potteries Phrases

Here is a little guide for outsiders visiting the area. A few key phrases they may need to get around The Potteries:

- What's your name? - Wot's thar neem yoth?
- Where are you from? – Weer at frum?
- Where is the nearest food place? – Cost get snappin' near ere?
- Do you have change for the bus? – Ast gorrenny cheenge fer the buzz?
- Where is the cinema? – Weers the flicks?
- Is there a McDonalds close by? – Weers the Maccies rind ere?
- Where is the town centre my good friend? – Weers the tine centre mar mayte?
- Please help me – Gizz ond yoth
- What time is the next bus – Wot tarms the buzz cum yoth?

Stoke-on-Trent National Garden Festival 1996

Most of us remember the Queen opening the Stoke-on-Trent National Garden Festival. It was the second of Britain's National Garden Festivals. It was held in the city from 1 May to 26 October 1986 on the now Festival Park site in Etruria.

Here are some facts you may not know...

1. The festival cost over £16 million to put on.
2. Andy Cunningham, star of Bodger and Badger was one of the mobile puppeteers at the festival.
3. Some of the site is still there and can be accessed via various points around Festival Park. Many of the sculptures can be seen around Stoke-on-Trent
4. Over 6,000 people now work in this area and the adjoining Etruria Valley.
5. The Royal Mail commissioned a special set of stamps and first day cover featuring the festival.
6. The Festival attracted 2,184,052 visitors in total.
7. The Stoke-on-Trent Garden Festival included: 87 themed gardens, the biggest sculpture display since 1951
8. An extremely rare *Dungeons and Dragons* module, "Up the Garden Path", was based on the Festival site; only about thirty copies are known to have survived.

Stoke-on-Trent
19
86
NATIONAL
GARDEN
FESTIVAL

Pot Quiz

All the answers are in the book, have you been paying attention?!

1. In what year did the Kismet restaurant open in Burslem?
2. What make of Whisky did Jimi Hendrix ask for in Hanley?
3. What was the name of the band that Coldplay supported at The Sugarmill?
4. What venue did Regimes become in Hanley?
5. In what year did Stoke City win the League Cup?
6. What local band did Squeeze support in their first gig outside London?
7. What was the score when Port Vale knocked Spurs out of the FA Cup in 1988?
8. Whose toupee fell off whilst performing at The Torch?
9. What DJ first brought Daft Punk to Staffordshire?
10. In what year did Oasis play the legendary Wheatsheaf gig?

(answers at end)

Terry's all-new Pottersaurus!!

Pete Conway (legendary local comedian):

"Local dialects are sadly disappearing. My father and his mates spoke to each other in a language that was barely recognisable as English! It is very important that dialects and the strangeness of some words are recorded for posterity. I hope you find the book both funny and informative.

As they say in Boslem....theyt luv eet!"

A GET ON - Someone who uses people

ACTING THE OIL CAN - To act daft

ACTUAL STOKE IN STOKE - Stoke town itself

AFE TARM - Half time

AFE ATE - Half Eight

AGEN - Against

AHRUNBAY - A genre of songs often asked for by people with no taste in music aka R'n'B

AKS - Ask

ALLAWEEN - Halloween

AN ALL - Sentence ender - 'and all'

'ANLEY - Hanley

ANYROAD (or ANYWEE) - Anyway

AR ICE - Our house

AR LANE - High Lane

ARDUL – Idle

ARE SHONNER – I shan't

ARK - Our kid

ARM - I'm

ARM GEEN BOG – I am off to relieve myself

ARMOFF - I am off (leaving)

ARN - On

ARNTEE - Auntie

ARSE CRAYM - Ice Cream, often eaten from a cornet

AST BAYN MATCH? - Have you been the football match?

AST SAY NIGHT? - A question often asked before you have 'fun teat'.

ASTHEE? - Have you?

AT COOTIN? - Are you courting? A phrase often heard at family gatherings when an elderly guest asks a youngster if they are seeing anybody currently?

AT GEEN ITE? - Are you going out?

ATNA? – Aren't you?

AV YA ON - (1) The offer of a fight. (2) play a joke on

AVEET - Have it

AVINGTON - The place where selfish people are said to hail from

AWEE - Away

AYZ – He is

BBC - Bucknall Bowling Club

BACK ROAD - Toilet

BACKY - A lift on the back of a bike

BAINS - Beans

BAGGERCRAP - A bag of crap

BANDIT COUNTRY - Term of endearment for Meir.

BANES – Most enjoyable on toast

BANK (or BONK) - Hill

BAP - Bun

BARK - Bike

BARRA - Barrow

BAS TED - A child sans father

BASTED BONK - Basford Bank

BATHPOO - Bath Pool, famous 'dogging' site.

BAY - Be

BAY CHUM SPIDERS - Beecham's Powders

BAYN - Been

BAYER - Beer

BAYPASS - Bypass

BAYT - Bite

BEREET - It will be alright

BEEPEEN - Beeping

BENTILEE DISCOUNT - Stolen

BIDDLE (or BIDDOW) - Biddulph

BIDDLEMOOR - Biddulph Moor

BIDDS - Used to be the place to dress up as a cowboy and line dance.

BIRRER - Bit of

BITE TARM - About time

BLACK OWER BILL'S MOTHERS - It's getting dark

BLART - To cry

BLERK - Bloke

BLOW – Blue

BLOW CLOCK - Meeting place in Hanley

BO - Ball

BO GRAIN - Ball Green

BOATCAKE - Getting a completely overloaded oatcake with all the ingredients available.

BOATS - Worn on your feet.

BOBBIN - To skive from school or work

BODDLEY GRAIN - Baddeley Green

BOG – Toilet

BONGEY NEET - Bonfire Night

BONK OLIDEE - Bank Holiday

BOOOOK - Book

BOSLEM - Burslem - The Mothertown

BOSTED - ugly, unsavoury in appearance

BOSTEEN - Dying for something, like a wee.

BOTHDEE - Birthday

BRADDA - Bradwell

BRASSOS - Brassingtons

BRICKEET - Soil oneself due to fear

BRIT - The Bet 365 Stadium formerly called The Britannia

BROK- In need of repair

BRUNT - Burnt

BUCK - A male animal and definitely not a book!

BUR CHAZE ED - Birches Head

BUY QUAIL - There are usually two of these on a cycle

BUZZ - Bus

CHUCKIN IT DINE - Raining

CONNOR EAR - What was that you said?

COO - Cow

CADGE - Beg

CANST – Can you

CANTY CANTY CUSTUD - A tell tale

CAR BOAT SEAL – Somewhere to get rid of you unwanted items, or pick up a bargain

CAR TOSS - Cart Horse. Rag & bone men used to have one of these.

CARLO - To be drunk

CAUSE THEE COST - Of course you can

CASSLE - Newcastle Under Lyme

CHAYKEE - Cheeky

CHAYZE - Cheese

CHEER – Pull one of these up and sit down

CHELP - Too much lip

CHES - Chesterton

CHEWBE - Tube

CHEWSDEE - Tuesday

CHICAGO ROCK - A pub that is neither Chicago themed or plays rock

CHONNUCK - Turnip

CHUNTER - To have a grumble

CLAY ED - What some outsiders refer to Stokies as.

CLEMMED (or CLEMT) - Hungry

CLOD - Lump of mud

CLODHOPPERS - Shoes

CLOZE - Clothes

CLOZE HOSS - What you put the washing on to dry it

COB ON (or COBBED) - In a mood

COCK'S ENTRY - An alley way in Boslem! What did you think it was you dirty beggar?

CODGE - Dodgy workmanship

CONE FLEEKS - Corn Flakes

CONNA - Can't

CONNA SPAYKE - Can't speak - the situation has left me lost for words

COOOOK - Cook

COOT - Coat

COOTIN - Courting (dating)

COST KICK A BO AGEN A WO AN YED IT TILL IT BOSTS? - Can you kick a ball against a wall and head it until it bursts?

COST – Can you?

COSTNA? – Can’t you?

COTT - Normacott

COW MOP - Mow Cop

COWD - Cold

COWNSLICE (or KINDSLICE) - Council house

CRANK CITY (or CRACK CITY) - Crackley

CRASH US A FAG? - Could you spare me a cigarette? (Smoking is bad for your health)

CRAYM - Cream

CROG - Kick

CUDNA - Could not

CUSTUD - Custard

CUT - Canal

DARN – Down

DAYED - Died

DAYLO - Dale Hall

DAY ROAD - The D Road

DECKEET - Stop it

DECKED - When someone has been knocked to the floor

DEE - Day

DEETH - Death

DICK SHUNREE – You can look up a word in one of these

DINE - Down

DINER KNIGHT - A homeless person

DITHER - To tremble or to waste time

DOCKERS - Doctor Marten shoes

DOFFERS - People who jump over walls

DOG MITHA - Trouble

DONAMAYT - What fills a doner kebab

DOOBERRYFIRKING - A 'thing'

DOODAH - Another 'thing'

DOOER - Door

DOOFA - Remote control

DRINE DEED- Drowned

DUCK - Term of endearment as in 'Big issue duck!'

DUNNA - Don't

DUNEET - It is done

DUST – Do you?

DUST NOO – Do you know?

EAT - It

EAT SITE - When something is no longer in.

ECKA - Nickname for anyone called Eric

EETITE - Perhaps a trip to McDonald's.

EE YAR - Here you go

EIGHT'S - It's

ENYTARM - Anytime

ENYWEE - Anyway

ENYWEER- Anywhere

ENYWUN- Anyone

ERNIE NUFF - To earn enough to survive

EY UP NAR - Hey up now.

FAG HAZE - Fegg Hayes

FANG - Catch or seize

FAR ROD NOMMER - Song, "If I Had a Hammer (The Hammer Song)" written by Pete Seeger and Lee Hayes. It was written in 1949 in support of the progressive movement.

FARN - Fine

FARVE - Five

FATE - Fight

FAYL - Feel

FAYT - Feet

FAYCEBOWK - Facebook

FAYTHER - Father

FAYUL - Feel

FEET - Fight

FENTELONA - Fenton, if it were to be twinned with Barcelona

FESTITUTE - A girl who hangs around Fezzy Park looking for boys with nice cars. AKA Carbike.

FESS - Face

FEZZY PARK - Festival Park

FINK - Think

FLEX - Reflex Bar

FLO ER - Floor

FLOOZY - A 'loose' woman

FLUMMOXED - Bothered

FOE STAYTH - False teeth

FOE BITS - Fall to bits

FOE DINE – To trip up and lose one's balance

FOLLER - Follow

FOOTBO (or FOOTEE) - Football

FOOTBO FOST - Football First

FORRED - Forehead

FOST - First

FUNT – Found

FUN TEAT – It has been located

FUR - Far

FOE - Fall

FOW - Full

FOOWER - For

FOWER - Four

FRAYBE - Freebie

FRAYZEEN - Freezing

FREEDEE - Friday

FRITTENED - Scared

FUNTEET - Often heard when something has been recovered.

GANSEY - Sweater/Jumper.

GARDEEN (or GARDIN) - Garden

GEEN – Going

GEEN ITE – Going out

GETHA - Together

GERROFFYA - I don't believe you

GHOSIS SITTIN ON POSIES EATIN BURRED CRUSSIES WITH THEIR FISSIES - Ghosts sitting on posts, eating crusts with their fist

GILLEREETH - Gillow Heath

GIVINTON - The place where generous people are said to hail from

GOO - Go

GOOIN RIND WRECKIN - Said when someone is making a story over long

GOO ARN - Go on

GOOIN - Going

GOOSE LOW - Go slow

GOREET - Got it

GRAY NICE – You can grow tomatoes in one of these glass structures

GRAIN - The colour you get when you mix yella and blueGRIND - Ground

GULLEY (or GINNEL) - Alley

GYP - Pain

HADNA - Had not

HARV - Hive

HELL HEATH - Another cute term for Chell Heath

HEE RAT - Here you go

HEROIN CROSS - Heron Cross

HERSEN - Herself

HIGH SIX - Popular greeting in the sticks

HIS SEN - His self

HOMMER - Hammer

HOPE STRATE - A place where legend says you could meet ladies of the night

HOPE STREET CAMO - Leopard print

HOSPICE - A kind of liquid often found in a stable.

HOSS - Horse

ICE - House

I'LL LOB A DUCKER AT THEE - I will throw a big brick at you

IDLE AS DEAN'S DOG - The epitome of idle

INTEET - Isn't it?

ITE - Anything

ITERTINER - Someone from a surrounding town visiting Stoke

JED - Dead

JEOWKIN - Joking

JETTY - Toliet

JIGGERED - Tired

JOJO TELL - The George Hotel

JOKE SH*TTY - What Port Vale fans call Stoke City

JONTY - Nickname for anybody who plays cricket with the surname Johnson

K NUTTON - Knutton without the silent 'k'

K NYPERSLEY - Knypersley without the silent 'k'

KALE - Housework

KAY - Key

KAYP (or KEYP or KEP) - Keep

KEGGY HANDED - Left handed

KETCH - Catch

KEYP ONTH BRICKS - Keep on the bricks

KICKABITE - Kickabout

KICKSCREW - Kidsgrove

KIDDA Mate or friend.

KILL– KilnKWAYE - Queen

L.A - Longton Area

LAID UP - Ill

LAKE - Leek

LARK - Like

LARME - Lime

LARM KILL BONK- Limekiln Bank

LART - Light

LIGGER - Liar

LIVING OVER THE BRUSH - Living in sin

LINER - Linesman (or woman)

LOB SCOUSE - Lobby

LOBBY - The most delicious stew - thick bread is a must to dip

LONG POWT - Longport

LOOOOK - Look

LOZZUCK (or LOZZOCK) - Unsupported laziness

LOW KITE – Look out

LOW KITE FER – Keep an eye out for, keep watch

LUCK SHREE – A state of great comfort or elegance

MARDARSE - A moody person

MACK - Make

MACKEES - McDonalds

MAIN - Mean

MAR - My

MARRA - Mate

MARL - Mile

MARLICE - Milehouse

MARN – Mine

MATE – Meat

MATE N TAYTER – Wrights make a delicious pie using these ingredients

MAY - Me

MAY BANKER - Stokie rhyming slang maybe?

MAY UN MAR LADY - Me and my lady

MESEN - Myself

MESS OFF! - Go away!

MIDDOPOTE - Middleport

MILL - The Sugarmill music venue

MITCH - The Michelin Tyre Company

MITHER - To bother

MIZOG - Miserable person

MOANEEN - Morning

MOLLY LEIGH - A Burslem woman who was accused of witchcraft, but died before being tried

MOOER (or MOWER) - More

MUNDEE - Monday

MUSTA - Must have

NAID - Need

NAR - Now

NARCE - Nice

NAYT (or NEET) - Night

NECK END - Longton

NESH - Someone who is rubbish in a cold environment. Unfired clay that's difficult to use.

NOGGER - Football

NOW TELL SIN - Nothing else in

NOWEEN MAY NOWEEN THAY - Popular Abba song - 'Knowing me, knowing you'

NOWT - Naughty person

O' ABITE - All about

OCKERED - Awkward

OFFY - The local place to buy booze and fags AKA The off licence

OFFEETSHEAD - Someone or something that acts a bit daft

OLIDEE - Holiday

ONEET - When one is well and truly 'On it' and top of their game.

ONE OFF EIGHT? – You have been challenged to a fight

ONNER - Are not

ONNERBITE - On about

OOER - Over as in 'She's had a few too many an is all ooer the shop!"

OOTCEEK - Oatcake (enough said)

ORATE - Are you alright?

OV - Have

OWAT - How are you?

OWAT ME OWD - How are you my old friend?

OWD or ODE - Old

OWD SPARCE - An aftershave favoured by men having a mid-life crisis.

OWE DICE - An old house - a property that has been standing for a good number of years

OWER - Over

OWE SKOO - A type of rave music - old school

PACE TRAYTEE - Signed at the end of the war.

PACEFULL - Peaceful

PAD LEEN – Walking in shallow water

PAPAL - More than one person

PARKHO - Park Hall - Also famous for its 'dogging'.

PEEDEE - Pay Day

PHRASE - For he's (as in 'phrase a jolly good fella')

PIG PEN - A former purveyor of fine ales, you could hav also bought cheap meats and unofficial sportswear in there if dodgy Bob was around.

PIKELET - The smaller cousin of the oatcake, often containing raisins or currants.

PLACE - Police

POBS - Bread and milkPOLICE - Place

POO - Pool

PORK T*TS - Nice name for Talke Pits

PORT FAIL - What Stoke City fans call Port Vale.

POT HERB - What some people from Leek call Stokies

POTTERS – Two-week holiday from when we had loads of Pot Banks - last week of June, first week of July.

POTTRAYS - (1) The Intu Shopping Centre in Hanley, formerly known as The Potteries Centre. (2) The Potteries (area)

POWTILL- Porthill

PUNCHER - Puncture

PUTHERY - A term to describe damp weather conditions.

QWAYNAGER - A yoth that likes the older lady, in the days of Queens in Basford.

QWAYNS - Queens - A former nightclub in Basford that was a popular 'grab a granny' venue.

RAINBOW CITY - The Coalville Estate in Weston Coyney was known as this in the 80s due to houses painted different colours.

RAMMEL - Scruffy animal

RARE N CROSS - Heron Cross

RATASSED - Inebriated

RAYDEEN - reading

RAYGENT - The Regent Theatre, the place to catch Jonny Wilkes in his annual panto.

RAYJO - Radio (6 Towns, Signal or Stoke)

RAY ZEENS – An essential ingredient in pikelets

REE SOSS - The likes of Red Rum

REET SPY - Wright's Pie

RAY TOOK - Can cause someone to be knocked to the floor

REGIMES ROMEO - Guy with a mullet, white shirt, white songs and slip on shoes who would try to chat your missus up in the popular 80s nightclub when you went to the loo.

RIND - Round

RIND A BITE - You can go around one in your car.

RISEN ON - Cold, well freezing actually!

ROBEESDAD - Pete Conway

ROCKS - Sweets

RON - Later on

ROT – Large rodent

SAFFOG - Somebody who is unclean, scruffy looking or generally smelly. Unpleasant things can be described as "Saffy"

SAGGER MAKERS BOTTOM KNOCKER - Saggars are used to hold and protect pottery during kiln-firing. It was someone's job to make the bottom of the saggar, by placing clay in a metal hoop and knocking it into shape.

SAN DOLE - Sand Hole - a recreational park in Gillow Heath

SANFER DILL - Sanford Hill

SATDEE - Saturday

SAYTHEE - See you later!

SCABBY ABBEY - Abbey Hulton's unfair alter ego

SCHOLESY - DJ and compere from Jollees

SCRAG END - Another nice name for Meir

SCRAN - Food

SCRAWNEE - Little

SCRAWP - Scrape or graze.

SCRATCH TOES - Sachmos Nightclub

SEAL - Sale

SEAL'S BROK - When, after a few beers the need to visit the loo increases.

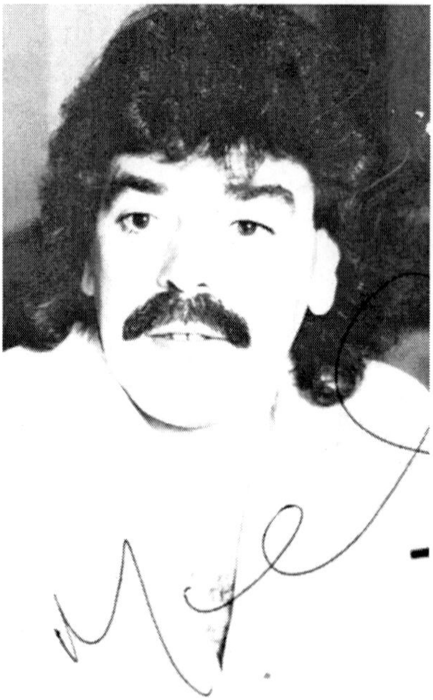

MEL SCHOLES

SEN - Self

SENATUCT - Lazy person

SENTNUL - Local newspaper

SEOWN - Soon

SHALEES - Shelly's Lazerdome - Popular rave spot in Longton in the late 80s/early 90s

SHARNT- Shall not

SHART- Shout

SHARTART - Shout out from DJ

SHEED - To spill liquid.

SHELLY'S GURN - A face adopted by people who have had it a bit too large.

SHOT A PINKER NITE - Give birth

SHOWND- To show

SHOWT – Short

SHUG- Term of endearment meaning 'sugar' as in 'A dozen oatcakes please shug!'

SHUDNA - Should not

SHY TICE - A place to relieve oneself

SHY TIGHT - Raise your voice louder still

SIDERDS - Sideways

SKINNY - Tight

SKOO - School

SLAPE (or SLAYP) - Sleep

SLAT - To throw

SMAIN - Do you know what I mean

SMOSHIN' - Smashing

SMO THONE - Smallthorne

SMO THONE BONK - Smallthorne Bank

SMO THONE RIND A BITE - Smallthorne roundabout

SMO TOKE – Small talk

SNADE GRAIN - Sneyd Green

SNEEP - To upset

SOOTY – Sooty (Not Sutty)

SOSS - Mate

SOUL-ON-TRENT - Self explanatory

SOTE - Salt

SPARCE - Spice

SPAY CUP - Talk louder

SPIKEY MAN - Jack Frost, lives on Debenhams wall

SPOCK - Spoke

SPUG - Sparrow

STAFFYSHER - How we say Staffordshire

STRAME – Small river

STOKE STOKE - So good they named it twice

STOKIE 1-2-3! - A game played in the playground where two teams take turns to catch each other.

STOKEYO DRIFT - Before the car cruising ban at Fezzy Park you would often see wannabe Paul Walkers in their souped up Fiestas.

STOKÉMON - Referring to some of the creatures that can be found in most of the 6 town centres... Gotta catch 'em all (well the police do)

STOPEET - Stop it

STOUKING - Sticking cup handles on

STROE - Straw

STROE YED - A person with light ginger hair

SUBWEE - Subway

SUNDEE - Sunday

SUT - Sat

SWATE - Sweet

TAB LEET – A hand-held version of a computer

TAK - Take

TARM - Time

TASH (or STASH) – Facial hair grown above the top lip

TAY - Tea

TAY BOG - Used with boiling water and a drop of milk, it can be quite refreshing.

TAY SPONE - used for stirring hot drinks

TAYDY - Tidy

TAYTER WAITER - Potato water

TAYTH - Teeth

TER - To

TERDEES - Today's

TERRY STICE - Terraced house

TESCO TWO STRIPES - Trainers in the 80s and 90s that looked like Adidas but had a stripe missing.

THAY KNOWST - Do you know

THE ABBEY - Abbey Hulton

THE DALE - Silverdale

THE LEE - Bentilee

THEE - You, as in 'Get thee sen darn Th' Playce!'

THEEYER - There

THOSDEE - Thursday

THRAY - Three

THRAY WHALER - Reliant Robin

THUT- That

TIFFS - Tiffany's Nightspot

TINTIN - It isn't in as in 'Have you been drinking again Jeff, tin tin yet!'

TITTENSOR - (1) A village near to Trentham (2) Jogger's nipple?

TIP ROT – Scavanger

TOE – Two

TOW RUM – Two of them

TOE CRATE - Talk right

TOE RATE- Are you alright?

TOKE- Talk

TOM TIT – (1) A number two (2) - Own, like 'on my own'. Tom Tit is a relative of Jack Jones.

TONTINE TWO STEP - A staggering alcohol fuelled walk often seen in Hanley.

TOOER- tour

TOP WUN, NARCE WUN - Top one, nice one

TOWAN - Town

TOWARZ - Alton Towers theme park

TRAPECING (or TRAIPSING) - Wandering

TRAYS – Birds often nest in these

TRAY ICE – Wooden structure built up in the branches

TRAY KULL – Treacle

TRENT VEGAS - Gambling capital of Stoke (online casinos mainly). Trent Vale.

TRYSERS - Trousers

TUNSTALL TORTILLA - Oatcake

TUNSTER - Tunstall

TURTS - Said when something really hurts

TUSHERS - Teeth

TUTHER - The other

TWENEE BENEE – A packet of Benson & Hedges

UN – And

UN OWE - Also

UNDERGROUND HERO - The guy with a lighter in the 'beer garden' of Unders

UNDERS - The Underground Nightclub

VALLIES - A 90s nightclub aka Valentinos

VAYUL - Port Vale

VICKY ROAD - The main road from 'Anley duck to Fenton - Victoria Road

VODAPIG - A worker at Vodafone

WAITER – Turn the tap on if you want a drink of this

WAITER FOE – Cascading liquid

WASS'S MARKET - A popular market in the 80s where the bus depot is now by the gasometer between Adderley green and Bentilee

WAYNE GEEN ITE – We are going out

WAYULZ - Wales

WEBSURT - Website

WEE - Way

WEE ITE - Exit

WEE RAT? - Where are you

WENSDEE - Wednesday

WENZEE TAK POLICE? - When does it take place?

WERRET - Worry

WESSER - Westport Lake

WHALE - Wheel

WHALE BARRA - Wheel barrow

WIKS - Weeks

WIMMIN - Women

WITHERS - Wetherspoons/ With us

WO - Wall

WO KEEN - Walking

WOM - Home

WOSS - Worse

WONNERMAY - Like the Shaggy song 'It wasn't me'

WONEET? - Wasn't it?

WONTEET - I want it

WORRANOB - Someone who is acting in a way that's unsavoury and out of order

WRONGUN - One who is wrong, an unsavoury character

WUDNA - Wouldn't

WURLD - World

WURLDY - Great goal

WUN - One (or When)

WUNNA - Won't

WUT? - Would you?

YART? - Are you out?

YED - Your head

YELLA - Yellow

YELP - Your help

YERCUT - Haircut

YORPING - Shouting

[Pot Quiz answers: 1962, Johnny Walker, Terris , Uropa, 1972, Climax Blues Band, 2-1, Arthur Connolly, Kelvin Andrews, 1994]

And finally...

The other week, I went to see a Robbie Williams gig and had to sit next to an insurance salesmen.

And through it all, he offered me protection!

INDEX